Contents

Introduction

Key: **FORT WILLIAM**   Station location

© Mike Heath 2016

First published in 2016

British Library Cataloguing in Publication Data

A catalogue record for this book is available from the British Library.

ISBN 978 1 85794 465 5

Silver Link Publishing Ltd
The Trundle
Ringstead Road
Great Addington
Kettering
Northants NN14 4BW

Tel/Fax: 01536 330588
email: sales@nostalgiacollection.com
Website: www.nostalgiacollection.com

Printed and bound in the Czech Republic

Back in the 1880s the people of Fort William and the fishermen to the west were frustrated at the lack of a rail connection. To the south, the Callander & Oban Railway had reached Oban. To the north, the Dingwall & Skye Railway had completed its line to Strome Ferry and was heading to the coast at Kyle of Lochalsh. At that time the railhead for Fort William was 50 miles to the east, at Kingussie, where the Highland Railway had opened a station in 1863. The vast expanse of beautiful, if wild, landscape between these lines was left remote and inaccessible to all but the most determined traveller.

After a long fight, the town finally got its own direct link to Glasgow when the North British Railway's line opened in August 1894. The railway promoters' original intention was to also construct a branch west of Fort William past Glenfinnan to the head of Loch Ailort, then turning down the southern shore to terminate at Roshven on the Sound of Arisaig. At Banavie a short branch was to be installed to a pier on the Caledonian Canal to connect with the steamers operating on the waterway. Unfortunately, among other problems, there were objections from a local landowner whose grand home would have overlooked the Roshven terminus and proposed pier. His concerns revolved around the potential disruption to his sporting estate by the influx of tourists! This was supported by Parliament, so the construction of the West Highland Railway 'extension' was limited to the branch to the Caledonian Canal at Banavie, which became the temporary western extent of the line.

A coastal link was still the target and attention turned to Mallaig Bay, 40 miles from Fort William, which was chosen as the site for a new port and railway terminal. This was envisaged as a difficult and expensive route to construct and it thus took two years to raise the necessary investment and obtain Parliamentary approval. Just before the first trains from Glasgow arrived in Fort William in August 1894 the West Highland Railway (Mallaig Extension) Act was passed by Parliament. The first sod was cut at Corpach on 21 January 1897 by Lady Margaret Cameron of Locheil, the wife of Cameron of Locheil, a staunch supporter of the 'extension'. Over the next four years builders constructed magnificent concrete viaducts over rivers and glens, floated the line across peat bogs, excavated 100 cuttings and tunnelled their way through some of the hardest rock in Britain. On 1 April 1901 the 'Mallaig Extension' was opened to traffic.

Thereafter the railway settled to the routine conveyance of local residents to and from Fort William, transporting tourists to the steamers waiting to ferry them to the Western Isles, and carrying the fish trawled from the sea to markets in the south. The Second World War saw an increase in traffic with a naval repair base set up at Corpach. The 1950s saw the introduction of Observation Cars on some services to attract even more tourists to witness the spectacular views from the line.

In the early 1960s British Railways deemed it uneconomic to continue to transport fish by rail and, while recommendations for the cessation of local services in the Beeching Report were refused, there were concerns for the railway's future. Salvation came in 1963 when a 22-year agreement was signed that would see a new paper mill at Corpach receive and dispatch materials by rail. This rejuvenated the line.

However, the 1980s saw an air of despondency return once more as the paper mill closed. But a change of approach by management, which oversaw the introduction of steam-hauled excursions in 1984, the simplification of operations with the introduction of single-manning of locomotives and a change to Radio Electronic Token Block signalling proved to be the start of recovery. Further savings were made by the introduction of diesel multiple units to replace the loco-hauled stock in 1988. As the railway celebrated its centenary in 2001 the future looked bright, and so it has proved to be.

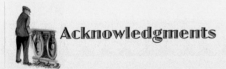

Acknowledgments

The Author would like to thank both the Glenfinnan Station Museum (John Barnes) and the Friends of the West Highland Line for their assistance in the preparation of this book. Both organisations offer more detailed information on the line and replicas of the posters reproduced in this book can be purchased from the museum shop at Glenfinnan.

Their contact details are as follows:-
- glenfinnanstationmuseum.co.uk
- www.westhighlandline.org.uk

FORT WILLIAM

The original station at Fort William was further west alongside Loch Linnhe at Station Square. This typically Scottish building featured a turret and a double-arched entrance serving its three platforms.

In 1975 it was demolished to make way for the Fort William bypass and the current grey concrete structure was opened by British Railways on 13 June 1975. It has recently been refurbished to improve passenger facilities.

Regular steam operations out of Fort William ceased back in 1962. However, they resumed in 1984 and every year since then there has been a summer steam-hauled passenger service between Fort William and Mallaig, making this the longest-established regular steam-hauled service in Britain.

Prior to 1994 operations were under the auspices of Scotrail and my own first visit was in 1993 when, advertised as 'The Lochaber', the train was in the hands of London Midland & Scottish Railway (LMS) Stanier Class 5 4-6-0 No 44767 *George Stephenson* (see title page). The locomotive looked pristine prior to departure from Fort William and the

INTERCITY
Nostalgic
Days Out by Steam
The Lochaber
from Fort William

Special Steam Hauled Excursions
for Summer 1993

Above left **FORT WILLIAM:** Going back in time to 31 May 1963 and to the original station at Fort William we find No D5357 having just arrived with a train from Mallaig.

Left **FORT WILLIAM:** Three days earlier sister locomotive No D5354 and No D8107 are in charge of the Mallaig to Glasgow service making a 1.25pm departure from Fort William. *Both SLP Archive, Ray Ruffell Collection*

Left **FORT WILLIAM:** On 18 September 1995 8F Class 2-8-0 No 48151 rests at Fort William depot. Built in 1942 No 48151 was withdrawn from BR service in January 1968 and sent to Dai Woodham's famous Barry scrapyard. Languishing there for over 8 years, No 48151 was purchased in 1975 and returned to full main-line working order in 1988. *Ray Ruffell*

trip included the usual stop at Glenfinnan.

From the summer of 1994 the Carnforth-based West Coast Railway Company has provided the carriages and train crews for what is today known as the 'Jacobite' operation, with locomotives, certified for main-line work, hired from private owners.

Right **GLENFINNAN:** Stanier Class 5 4-6-0 No 44767 *George Stephenson* hauling 'The Lochaber' makes the stop referred to above.

Above **FORT WILLIAM:** A regular provider of locomotives is Riley & Son from Bury in Lancashire, and Ian Riley's 'Black Five' 4-6-0 No 45407 *The Lancashire Fusilier* has been a regular performer on 'The Jacobite' trains for many years. Here it waits alongside the platform at Fort William on a very sunny June morning in 2012. *Karl Heath*

Right **FORT WILLIAM:** As the train accelerates away from Fort William it passes over Mallaig Junction, where the line to Glasgow diverges, before getting into its stride alongside the sidings on the approach to Lochy Bridge. *Karl Heath*

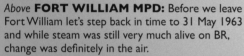

Lochy Bridge

Above **FORT WILLIAM MPD:** Before we leave Fort William let's step back in time to 31 May 1963 and while steam was still very much alive on BR, change was definitely in the air.

In the first image 4F 0-6-0 No 44255 is the duty 'snow engine'. Those who remember the winter of 1963 will know how busy this loco would have been that year.

In the second image 'J37' Class 0-6-0 No 64636 in the company of fellow 'J37' No 64592 stand outside Fort William shed having been sent to haul the Fort William to Mallaig section of the Scottish Locomotive Fund's 'Jacobite' rail tour, which started and finished at Glasgow Queen Street on 1 June 1963. Interestingly, both locomotives were declared unfit to bring the tour back from Mallaig and Bo-Bo Class 2 No D5351 was called on to stand in.

The third image shows 'rescuer' No D5351 in the company of No D5356 at Fort William the day before the tour. *All Ray Ruffell*

The original branch, which was ultimately extended to Mallaig, initially ran to a pier on the Caledonian Canal at Banavie, and opened in June 1895, a year after the main line had reached Fort William. This delay was mainly due to the difficulties in constructing the viaduct over the River Lochy. The foundations for the masonry piers that carry the four 80-foot spans consist of cast-iron cylinders sunk well into the river bed.

Below **LOCHY BRIDGE:** No 45407 crosses the viaduct in June 2012. Note that the main track decking is attached half-way up the main girders; this is unusual, as elsewhere on the West Highland line the deck is on the top! *Karl Heath*

Above **LOCHY BRIDGE:** Another regular performer, also from the Riley & Son stable, is 'Black Five' No 44871, seen crossing the river on a much cooler morning in October 2010.

Observation Coach Train at Lochy Viaduct near Fort William

THE WEST HIGHLAND LINE

SEE BRITAIN BY TRAIN

BANAVIE

Banavie was the western extent of the West Highland line until the extension to Mallaig was opened in 1901. Here the railway had to cross the Caledonian Canal and a massive steel bowed-truss swing bridge was constructed.

Left **BANAVIE:** No 45407 returns the steam whistle acknowledgement from the 1943-built coal-fired 'Clyde Puffer' *VIC 32* as it eases over the swing bridge. The 'Clyde Puffers' were once a vital supply link around the west coast of Scotland and the Hebrides. *VIC 32* is one of only two coal-fired examples in preservation and can often be seen on leisure cruises in the area.

Above **BANAVIE:** No 44871 crosses with a return train to Fort William on 5 October 2010. *Karl Heath*

Below and right **BANAVIE:** Both the railway and road bridge open simultaneously when required as here to allow *VIC 32* to pass through into the bottom lock of Neptune's Staircase, a series of eight locks that is the longest staircase lock in Great Britain. Built by Thomas Telford between 1803 and 1822, it takes around 90 minutes for a boat to ascend the 64-foot rise.

CORPACH

From Banavie the railway passes through a cutting before arriving at Corpach. Here is the western sea entrance of the Caledonian Canal, where it connects with Loch Linnhe via three locks. With the canal opening in 1822, the village grew in the mid-19th century in response to the introduction of large steamers using the canal, linking Inverness with Glasgow. A naval repair base was established during the Second World War, the site of which was later redeveloped for a pulp mill that was a major employer in the area until closure in 1980.

The landscape surrounding the canal and shoreline at Corpach is spectacular, not least the superb views across to Fort William and Ben Nevis.

Below and right **CORPACH:** This is also a popular location for photographers. From the sea lock looking across the water, the train can be followed heading along the sea wall. On 10 October 2010 'Black Five' No 44871 was in charge.

Beside Loch Eil

On leaving Corpach the line passes through an industrial section once dominated by the paper mill, before emerging loch-side at Loch Eil Outward Bound halt, the only new station built since the line's opening. This basic halt was constructed, under Scotrail supervision, by young people from the nearby adventure centre that it now serves. It opened on 20 April 1985.

Loch Eil Outward Bound Halt

Above right and right **LOCH EIL OUTWARD BOUND HALT:** For many years there was just one 'Jacobite' steam service each day, leaving Fort William around 10.20am with the return service departing from Mallaig just after 2.00pm. In 2011, to meet an ever-increasing demand, West Coast Railways introduced a second train that departs around 2.30pm and crosses with the returning morning train at Glenfinnan. For the 2012 services No 44871 was rostered on most of these later trains and is seen approaching and passing over the crossing by the halt. *Both Karl Heath*

FASSFERN: One of the many hamlets dotted along the side of Loch Eil is Fassfern, located at the bottom of Glen Suileag. In October 2010 the trees lining the adjacent A830 road provided an autumnal backdrop as No 44871 scurried past.

LOCHEILSIDE

The next station is at Locheilside, which is a request stop serving the few houses scattered around this sparsely populated area. However, workshops and a pier were erected here when the line was under construction. But for the trees that line the track, the area would boast some outstanding views across the loch.

LOCHEILSIDE: The best views of this section of the railway are from the opposite bank alongside the A861 road, which follows a circuitous route along the south shore. From various locations it is possible to follow the progress of the train as it meanders along the bank of the loch, emerging from behind tree-lined sections at regular intervals, as seen here on the breezy morning of 14 October 2014.

Below **THE 'WETLANDS':** The flat land beyond the head of the loch is colloquially known as the 'Wetlands' for obvious reasons. Climbing away from this area and out of the woods, No 44871 is about to cross the A830 on the approach to Glenfinnan.

Above **LOCHEILSIDE:** Typical of Scotland, no two days offer the same conditions. This is the view on a very still morning in August 2014.

Glenfinnan Viaduct

The most famous structure on the West Highland line, the Robert McAlpine-built mass concrete Glenfinnan Viaduct is 416 yards long, comprises 21 arches, carries the railway across the valley of the River Finnan, and at its tallest stands 100 feet above the water. It took four years to construct between 1897 and 1901. It is now of course recognised all over the world, having 'starred' in a number of the 'Harry Potter' movies.

Left: **GLENFINNAN VIADUCT:** As the train descends towards the viaduct, the brakes have to be applied for the 25mph speed restriction over the structure.

Above: **GLENFINNAN VIADUCT:** The view from the River Finnan.

Right: **GLENFINNAN VIADUCT:** The viewing platform accessed via a steep roughly stepped climb behind the Glenfinnan Monument Visitor Centre reveals a magnificent panoramic view of McAlpine's stunning structure.

Left **GLENFINNAN VIADUCT:** No matter what the season, as the train eases across the viaduct passengers are treated to what must be one of the finest views from any railway in the world – the Glenfinnan Monument and the mountain-flanked Loch Shiel beyond. The monument was erected in 1815 to mark the vicinity where the Jacobite Standard was raised in 1745 to signal the start of the uprising led by Prince Charles Edward Stewart.

Opposite and following two pages **GLENFINNAN VIADUCT:** What is not always apparent when viewed from the main road and visitor centre is the tightly curved nature of the viaduct, which was built to a radius of 792 feet.

Below **Nr GLENFINNAN:** The next section of line, up to Glenfinnan station, climbs at gradients of 1 in 45 and 1 in 50, so the locomotive has to work hard, creating a sound affect that resounds across the valley.

Below **Nr GLENFINNAN:** The origins of St Mary & St Finnan's Catholic Church date back to the 1860s, although the building was constructed between 1870 and 1872.

GLENFINNAN

Opened on 1 April 1901, Glenfinnan station, with its two platforms, provides the first passing loop since Mallaig Junction back in Fort William. Today it continues to serve the local community and the ever-increasing number of tourists drawn to the area.

MALLAIG

Morar

Bracara

Loch Nevis

Tarbet

Loch Morar

A830

Arisaig

Glenfinnan Viaduct

Borrodale Tunnel

Beasdale Tunnels

Beasdale

Loch Nann Uamh Tunnels

Loch Nann Uamh

Polnish Tunnels

Lochailort

A830

Loch Eilt

Lochailort Tunnel

Loch Dubh

A830

Glenfinnan Viaduct

Leachabhuich
Tunnel

Glenfinnan

Tunnel

Polnish

Loch Sheil

Corpach

Loch Arkaig

Loch Eil

To Fort Agustus

Loch Lochy

Lochy Bridge

A82

Spean Bridge

NORTH BRITISH RAILWAY AND ITS COMMUNICATIONS

A82

Kinlocheil

Loch Eil Outward Bound Halt

Loch Eil

Corpach

Banavie

Torlundy

Loch Eil

Mallaig Junction

Original station

FORT WILLIAM

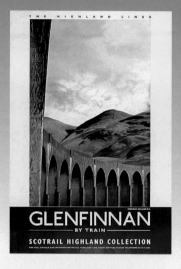

Above right **GLENFINNAN:**
Across the car park are two
refurbished carriages; one provides
sleeping accommodation while the
other is a cafe that, throughout the main season, serves
delicious homemade meals.

Above far right and right **GLENFINNAN:** The station
building houses the Glenfinnan Station Museum, with
exhibits illustrating the construction, impact and
operation of the Fort William to Mallaig line in the late
19th century. The booking office has been restored,
complete with the original tablet instruments, as has the
signal box at the end of the platform.

Shlatach Burn and the line's summit

On leaving Glenfinnan the locomotive has to tackle an unbroken 2½-mile climb to the line's summit, the watershed between Loch Sheil and Loch Eilt.

Nr GLEFINNAN: 'K1' No 62005 has just left Glenfinnan station and passed beneath the A830 road bridge in October 2009.

THE WESTERN HIGHLANDS
TRAVEL BY L·N·E·R
ASK FOR 'THE HOLIDAY HANDBOOK" AT BOOKSELLERS AND L·N·E·R AGENCIES (PRICE 6ᵈ

Below **SHLATACH BURN:** No 62005 is well on its way on a glorious summer's day in August 2014.

Right **SHLATACH BURN:** The last week of 'The Jacobite' in 2012 gave photographers some wonderful weather conditions. Fortunately my son Karl was on hand to record the West Highland Extension line in all its colourful glory.

Above and opposite **SHLATACH BURN:** The climb to the summit follows the meandering course of the Shlatach Burn and runs alongside the A830 'Road to the Isles'.

Loch Eilt

From the summit, the line dives through two of its 11 tunnels and winds its way down the tree-covered mountainside at gradients of about 1 in 50 for 2½ miles before emerging from the trees to be greeted with the stunning vista across Loch Eilt.

Opposite **LOCH EILT:** No 61994 *The Great Marquess* (facing Fort William) performs run-pasts during a photographers' charter along the eastern shore in October 2014.

Above: **LOCH EILT:** At Loch Eilt railway and road take opposite shores, and this view of 'Black Five' No 45407 charging along the southern shore was taken from the roadside. In the shadows, above the last carriage, is the Essan Bothy. Bothies are small huts or cottages for housing farm labourers or for use as mountain refuges; they are usually left unlocked and are available for anyone to use free of charge.

THE WESTERN HIGHLANDS
TRAVEL BY L.N.E.R.
FULL INFORMATION FROM ANY L.N.E.R OFFICE OR AGENCY.

At the western end of the loch there is a causeway that is a superb location for photography, albeit a bit of a trek from the road!

THE JACOBITE

Below **LOCH EILT:** On 21 August 2014 No 44871 was captured in a shaft of sunlight.

Above **LOCH EILT:** For the October 2014 photo charter with *The Great Marquess*, the weather could not have been better.

Lochailort to Loch Nan Uamh Viaduct

LOCHAILORT

Having curved round the end of Loch Eilt the train now climbs towards Lochailort, which has been unfavourably described as 'no more than a place name with a telephone kiosk'! The truth is that this charming hamlet, whose origins dates back to 1650 when the existence of an inn was recorded, has a lot more to offer, not least an interesting history. As part of the war effort in May 1940, Inverailort House was requisitioned by the War Office for a Special Training Centre as part of Combined Operations before being taken over by the Royal Navy in 1942 for the rest of the war.

LOCHAILORT: The train has just passed Lochailort station and is heading for another summit by the white chapel at Polnish.

Right **POLNISH:** The 'K1' heads a 'Jacobite' service on a much better October day two years later.

The white chapel at Polnish, or 'Our Lady of The Braes Roman Catholic Church' to give it its correct title, was built in 1872 but sadly has had no regular services since 1964.

Right **POLNISH:** No 44871 performs run-pasts during a damp and dismal photo charter in October 2011.

From the Polnish summit there is another steep drop at 1 in 50 as the train runs around Loch Dubh (the Black Loch). During the line's development the railway builders dammed this loch to feed a turbine to power the rock drills used to drive through the course of the 'extension'.

Above: **LOCH DUBH:** No 44871 heads back to Fort William with the 8 October 2010 service.

LOCH NAN UAMH:
Spanning Loch nan Uamh (the Loch of the Caves) is another splendid mass concrete viaduct built by Robert McAlpine. While Loch nan Uamh Viaduct is less spectacular than that at Glenfinnan, the sea view gives passengers their first glimpse of the shores of the Atlantic Ocean.

LOCH NAN UAMH: On 22 August 2014 the return afternoon service crosses the viaduct in evening sunshine.
In the distance the shaded slopes of Druim Fiaclach create a sinister backdrop.

A 1½-mile stretch at a gradient of 1 in 48 now follows as the line winds its way through woods, past rock outcrops and through tunnels as Beasdale Bank is tackled.

BEASDALE

Left **BEASDALE:** 'K1' No 62005 barks up Beasdale Bank on 12 October 2014.

Above **BEASDALE:** The same locomotive passes Beasdale station, which was built initially as a private station for the owner of Arisaig House. *Karl Heath*

ARISAIG

The station at Arisaig is the furthest west on Britain's railways, and a second passing loop allows trains to cross here. The signal box has been disused since the line became radio-controlled in 1987. However, the station buildings were refurbished in 2009 by the Railway Heritage Trust, Highland Rail Partnership and HiTrans.

Left and above **ARISAIG:** No 45407 *The Lancashire Fusilier* approaches the station and pauses on a clear 30 July 2012.

Beyond Arisaig and its view across to Loch nan Ceall, the line swings north, passing the furthest-west point of any railway in the British Isles near Kinloid.

Right **KINLOID:** With the islands of Eigg and Rhum darkening the horizon, Mallaig-bound No 62005 works round the curve at Kinloid on 12 October 2014.

Below **KINLOID:** On that same day the return working was hauled by 'K4' No 61994 *The Great Marquess*.

MORAR

After Kinloid is passed, the line heads for Morar, crossing the River Morar on its way. Here Robert McAlpine (nicknamed 'Concrete Bob') built a three-arch viaduct carrying the single track over the B8008 road as well as the river.

Below **MORAR:** On 25 August 2014 'K1' No 62005 put on this impressive display as it crossed the river.

MORAR: With Morar station just a few steam beats away, the passengers look out over stunning views of the white sands for which the area is famous.

The 'Road to the Isles' has been improved and upgraded over the years. At Morar the A830 was diverted to bypass the village, and although much of the old road has returned to nature, its route, much closer to the railway, is still evident in the landscape.

Below **MORAR:** Stanier-designed 'Black Five' Class No 45407 *The Lancashire Fusilier* passes Morar under sunny skies.

Right **MORAR:** 'K4' No 61994 *The Great Marquess* runs alongside the course of the old road as it too passes Morar but under leaden skies.

MALLAIG

The final approach to Mallaig brings the railway into close contact with the Atlantic for the first time, with undisturbed views of the Western Isles. This seaside terminus once boasted an attractive station with canopied platforms, a single-road engine shed, a steam crane for coaling locomotives and extensive sidings to deal with the considerable fish traffic that had attracted the railway in the first place. Nowadays there is a much simpler functional building, but thankfully the run-round loop remains for 'The Jacobite' trains and other steam-hauled excursions.

A t Mallaig visitors can soak up the atmosphere of a working fishing port, the main commercial operation on the West Coast of Scotland. For travellers it is a great base to explore the area and a gateway to the Isle of Skye and the Western Isles. Scheduled ferry services operate throughout the year.

Passengers on 'The Jacobite' have a couple of hours to explore this fascinating village, visit the Heritage Centre and take in a meal, usually locally caught fish and chips. Meanwhile the steam locomotive will have run round and been prepared for the return journey on what is justifiably marketed as one of the world's Greatest Rail Journeys.

Right **MALLAIG HARBOUR:** The line once extended to a concrete breakwater that had been built as part of the railway infrastructure. Fish and other goods could be loaded directly into railway wagons on the quay ready to be taken south or off-loaded for shipping to the isles.

The steam crane No PS/1268/5 is seen here at work on 27 May 1963. *SLP Archive, Ray Ruffell Collection*

The locomotives

Over the years there have been a variety of locomotives spending their summers on the West Highland line, and here are just the few that appear in this book. With the exception of No. 44767, they represent those that have been working on the line over the last few years.

Above: LMS Stanier Class 5 4-6-0 No 44767 was built at Crewe in 1947 and is unique in that it was constructed with some experimental features including outside Stephenson Link motion, a double chimney and Timken roller bearings. In preservation it has carried the name *George Stephenson*, and is currently out of service at the Midland Railway Centre.

Above left: Another 'Black Five', No 45407 *The Lancashire Fusilier* emerged from Armstrong-Whitworth in Newcastle in 1937. After many years working in the Midlands it was finally moved north and withdrawn from Lostock Hall shed in 1968. Since 1997 it has been owned by Ian Riley, from Bury, who restored it with a new tender with increased water capacity and fitted all the necessary safety equipment required to allow it to haul trains on the national network.

Left: A second Ian Riley-owned Class 5 is No 44871, another product of Crewe Works in 1945. This locomotive took part in the last BR steam-hauled rail tour on 11 August 1968, double-heading with No 44781 on the return leg (Carlisle to Manchester Victoria) of the Liverpool to Carlisle and back 'Fifteen Guinea Special'.

Left: LNER Thompson/Peppercorn Class 'K1' 2-6-0 No 62005 was built by the North British Locomotive Company in Glasgow in 1949. The 'K1s' worked all over the LNER, predominantly in the North East of England and on the West Highland line. After withdrawal in 1967 it was initially bought privately to provide a spare boiler for 'K4' No 61994. As this was not ultimately needed it was donated to the then infant North Eastern Locomotive Preservation Group, which restored the loco and maintain it to this day.

Below: The LNER 'K4' 2-6-0 locomotives were designed by Sir Nigel Gresley for use on the steeply graded West Highland line. No 61994 *The Great Marquess* was outshopped from Doncaster Works in 1937. After nationalisation in 1948 more powerful locomotives were moved up to the Fort William line and the 'K4s' were transferred to the Glasgow area. No 61994 spent its latter years on goods workings in Fife. Privately owned, the locomotive is currently out of service awaiting a major overhaul.